A Dementia Carer Poems

A Dementia
Carer Poems

Poems from the Heart for Caregivers

T.J. Hübner

A Dementia Carer Poems

A Dementia Carer Poems

Dementia Carer Poems
© Copyright 2020
T.J. Hübner (nom de plume)
All rights reserved
First published in the UK by Self-Published

A Dementia Carer Poems

Dedicated to my dearly departed father John who was the inspiration and frustration behind my writing.
(07/04/1931 – 02/06/2019)

In memory of my dearly departed mother Joan who we lost before her time.
(18/11/1937 – 24/04/2003)

A Dementia Carer Poems

Kneel before them,
Hold their hands,
Look into their eyes,
Tell them they are loved,
And not alone.

Do the above daily, so that your loved one
who has dementia knows you care, God bless.

Contents Page

A Dementia Carer Poems

Contents Page

A Dementia Carer Poems

A Dementia Carer Poems

Introduction

In 2014 after deciding to become the full time caregiver for my father, I was starting to feel isolated so I enrolled on a creative writing course with the local college which led to me joining a writing group where I learnt more about writing forms especially poetry.

In this group my confidence grew helping me share my poetry with other people. I started using poetry as a release to express the emotions I was feeling on a daily basis due to caring for an elderly parent with dementia.

I decided to use the power of poetry to express in words what I witnessed dementia doing to my father every hour of every day as well as the effect it had on myself.

The following poems are a selection of my writing which I have compiled over a seven year period whilst performing the role of caregiver. My hope is that the poems when read by other people help them to understand better what dementia does to the person diagnosed with it and empathise with them and their caregivers.

I also hope that any caregivers who may read these poems understand they are not alone in their endeavours to create a better life for people afflicted and that everyone at some point feels down hearted. I know what you go through each day, so let me say thank you in advance for reading my book, but also for doing what you do, a thankless task with only the reward of knowing you helped someone.

A Dementia Carer Poems

A Bygone Era

The mind returns to a bygone era
A young person in a childhood home
Unable to remember any other place
The only address the memory holds

Unaware of day, date or year
Hours, minutes and seconds a blur
A watch on the wrist to help
The concept of time a miss

A dilemma is in the eyes
Appearing blank and distant
There is still love hidden
Shown in emotional twinkles

Irritability and nervousness
All the signs of paranoia
Caused by the dementia
A families torment and woe

The body of a pensioner
A mind trapped in time
Youthful memories escaping
Sorrowful tears a flow

Alone

When you're a carer alone
It's a journey of the unknown
Not knowing what is in store
With every new daily chore

When you're a carer alone
Running around like a drone
It doesn't pay to be unhealthy
For life can become scary

When you're a carer alone
An existence that is on loan
A feeling of mindless solitude
Emotions hidden and subdued

When you're a carer alone
Your time is never your own
Always required and needed
Them before you, preceded

When you're a carer alone
Remember when you moan
No one forced you to agree
To give up being care free

When you're a carer alone
Just resolve, but not groan
As you do what you can
With an ever changing plan

When you're a carer alone
Have nothing for to atone
You care out of tenderness
With a mind of reverence

Black Hole

The brain under stress
Life in constant distress
Over rights and wrongs
Or what really belongs

The mind in upheaval
With thoughts, primeval
Nature in fluctuation
Causing frustration

The psyche in doubt
Should I bailout
Enough is enough
Reality getting tough

The sanity fractured
Sensibility tattered
Futures unknown
Needing to be a clone

The spirit disheartened
Clarity now darkened
Wishing for a lost childhood
Floating along as driftwood

The body tired and drained
A will to carry on strained
With black eyes so lifeless
In front, a feeling so mindless

The decision to love and care
Is an instinct, but be aware
For dementia destroys the soul
Creating a heartless black hole

Blood of His Blood

Life in turmoil over decisions
How to carry on without revisions
Do I blunder on out of love?
Or cut the strings and fly like a dove

A child's regard for a parent
Who is hardly coherent
Slowly feeling over stressed
Trying not to become depressed

Agonising over what is right
For both parties in this blight
How dad is, is not his fault
His abilities trapped in a decaying vault

I still see a strong independent man
Trying still to do whatever he can
With a body and Mind no longer his own
But not knowing it is letting him down

My love and respect for this person
Who took care of me without a reason
Other than I am blood of his blood
Gives me the reason to repay, understood

But how can we count the cost of caring
Without carrying on and never declaring
That this role reversal of parenthood
Where son becomes father is no good

Becoming an emotional rollercoaster
That is not advertised on any poster
This I do out of love as any child would
For I am the blood of his blood

Blues

When the mind is in the blues
And the future yields no clues
Year after year has passed
Lost memories are amassed
While the brain misleads
Life continues and proceeds

Their eyes look on in wonder
But behind thoughts are asunder
Not knowing what is even real
The past now appearing surreal
While the present consists of lapses
As memory continually collapses

Words and logic are a mystery
Life returns to protohistory
Knowledge of the simplest tasks
In time become the hardest asks
Now one's existence is unsecured
Cerebral pathways forever obscured

A way of life slowly decaying
As flashbacks are playing
Through a crumbling mentality
Whilst killing off the personality
And trapping one's individualism
In a realm of forced isolationism

Their world cascading uncontrollably
Unable to contribute socially
Never knowing their true plight
As they have no genuine insight
To the changes within their identity
Which disrupts the peaceful serenity

Burden Bearer

The essence of a carer
Is to be the burden bearer
To show the person empathy
And help them with their clarity
Assist them when it is required
Through love this is inspired

It is not to be taken lightly
Because to put it politely
This is a thankless task
For which you need a mask
While you cry inside
Put a smile on outside

The thing to remember
Is as a family member
You still require support
To prevent and thwart
Your very own demise
So learn to compromise

And as the burden bearer
Learn to be a sharer
Ask for some assistance
To keep a sane existence
While looking after a loved one
Till their days are finally done

A Dementia Carer Poems

Carer's Chain

Life is a constant struggle
Inside a virtual bubble

Living with an expectation
Of some great salvation

To release me from purgatory
As my life is totally nugatory

Trapped in a revolving hell
Which will not end I can tell

Until society can find a cure
That can remove and assure

The burdens of dementia carers
Who have no other sharers

So that I can shout out a plea
"Please let these chains no longer bind me"

Holding my mortal being in transition
With no possible means of fruition

Days and nights in distinct pain
While shackled in a carer's chain

Daily Routine

A daily routine helps reassure
As the disease begins to mature
Keeping the mind focused
Away from total psychosis

Repeating a day to day task
Along with questions to ask
Will keep the brain active
And the thoughts proactive

Setting times for the basics
Along with total patience
And a loving gentility
Gives attention stability

Having a pictorial memory
Helps the conscious journey
To rebuild their identity
Along with a unique entity

Dementia removes abilities
Along with their capabilities
How they deal with this adversity
Depends on the carer's diversity

Darkness of the Night

In the darkness of the night
What is seen will cause a fright
From the shadows it appears
The mind's eye creating fears

As the memories slip away
Concentration begins to stray
The simplest tasks found hard
A psyche that becomes scarred

With this illness of destruction
Creating an invisible abduction
As if one's life never existed
What is and what was, now twisted

Time no longer running as days
All the seasons out of phase
Hours and minutes unaligned
Brain patterns duly unassigned

From the depths of a thought
A glimmer of hope caught
Maybe a slight recollection
Then once again rejection

The lucidity of the mind
Complicates as if blind
Dementia taking control
Of the body and soul.

Dementia Woe's

The day started off so well
Then his dementia rang the bell
Boredom through the roof
Swell day gone poof

Mind set on one track
Creating a life so black
Simplest things complicated
The brain becoming dilapidated

Uncertainty at the forefront
Scared of living, so blunt
Both sufferer and carer drained
Locked in life equally constrained

Frustrated feeling overwhelms
As if trying to exist in two realms
Separated by the brains hemisphere's
Causing decidedly prickly atmosphere's

Is it wrong to carry on the tasks?
Hiding behind the smiling masks
Would it be better to say I give in?
Before life is truly in the bin

A Dementia Carer Poems

Final Tick

The burdens of time
Do no longer chime
Clock hands stick
Life takes a final tick

No more seasonal cheer
Just worries and fear
As the memory disappears
Along with countless tears

Trying to break the mould
By casting out the old
And ringing in the new
Cannot help these poor few

Stuck in an ever decreasing circle
While forgotten memories recycle
With thoughts that constantly sway
Through a mind under decay

Minutes of total lucidity
When their life has validity
Hours of absent mindedness
With uncontrollable nervousness

Their family become faceless
Words and actions graceless
Discussions sound gobbledygook
Without a type of reference book

This is what transpires
As the aging mind expires
The body may still be willing
But dementia is doing the killing

A Dementia Carer Poems

Groundhog Day

As time ticks by
My mind a blank
Undecided what to do
Reality a blur

Life goes at a crawl
Days never end
Repeated over and over
As if a nightmare

Minutes slip away
Emotions in turmoil
Seconds appear as hours
Subconscious dreaming

Tugged awake harshly
From a deep slumber
Alarm ringing continuously
Indicating a new dawn

Rubbing tired eyes
Stretching weary muscles
Fuelling the body
Restarting Groundhog Day

This is the life chosen
To honour the bond
Between father and son
That dementia destroys

A Dementia Carer Poems

Heads or Tails

Two sides of a coin dislodging
Past and present colliding
Reality and memory unfolding
A sense of loss cascading
The fear so debilitating
Dementia acting upon the aging

Is it heads or is it tails
Who knows what it entails
Either good or bad
Neither happy nor sad
A flip of the coin deciding
Dementia acting upon the aging

From birth to death we gamble
Through life we quickly amble
Till the day does dawn
That our mind is warn
The gamble is not paying
Dementia acting upon the aging

Soon everything is a concession
Life becomes an endless depression
The simplest things an obsession
In a way a form of expression
The failing mind self-raging
Dementia acting upon the aging

Hurt

The recesses of the mind
Occupy a space redefined
While the vision perceived
Is one of being deceived?

The ache the heart feels
Is how the body reveals
A loss the psyche conceals
Over the hurt that it seals

While outwardly the scene
That is portrayed and seen
Is not completely the truth
As the mind reverts to youth

Whether right or wrong
Hearing an old song
Can trigger a thought
Or create distraught

Days with very little chatter
Silence in the grey matter
When there is discussion
There is misinterpretation

Living a life of obsession
Controlled by depression
A memory in regression
With lots of concession

Remembering what was
The mind on pause
Not knowing what is
The life that was his

No longer anger or pain
In the decaying brain
No regrets of a life now gone
Due to the dementia spawn

I Only Ask One Thing

Consider who I am
Remember how I was
For I am still that person
Even if my body and mind is frail

Consider how you were treated
Reflect on how you treat me
For I only ask one thing
Understand with patience

Consider the loss I feel daily
Not being able to remember
A mist forms in the mind
To obscure the memory

A mind that is clouded
But a person that's the same
The way I act, I cannot help
Just love me till my life is done

In The Dark

When people say we understand
They cannot perceive the demand
How caring for a loved one
With dementia is not fun.

It requires the patience of a saint
Who can amplify their restraint?
While providing love and support
And not letting everything contort

So when those in the dark
About this illness, so stark
Voice their unguided opinions
I merely class them as minions

Individuals who never see the truth
And explaining is like pulling a tooth
For this nasty reaction of the mind
Is still a mystery to mankind

A Dementia Carer Poems

Insomnia

Time to relax, but unable to sleep
My mind in turmoil, I cry and weep
Tossing and turning, wide awake
Heart and soul under quake

A brain under pressure, total stress
Memories hold up in a cerebral recess
Thoughts preventing rem snoozing
Even when my body is bloody choosing

A mighty battle, my mind does fight
The body is weary, weak to the plight
Unable to defend against evil and all its might
Instead of shutting down to dream, I am in a fight

Incapable of rest, a never ending insomnia
In a complex mind scramble of anoxia
Asking questions of myself, subconsciously
That I wouldn't dare say out loud, consciously

Each night I face my fear, live and die with it
Until my anxiety is overwhelmed and split
Waking the next morning, reborn to fear no more
Till my head hits the pillow to restart the chore.

Outlandish scenarios on the mind
Both of us methodically entwined
His dementia affecting, my mind as well
Clattering around, like an alarm bell

A Dementia Carer Poems

Let Us Remember

Never say that war is good
For there is only spilt blood
Through the never ending cycle
That waring old foe's recycle

Which have gone on forever
In the ultimate endeavour
To create a planetary peace
But maybe never will cease

So on this day let us remember
Every fallen family member
Those who will never grow old
Be thankful for they enrolled

With honour they served
Their sacrifice forever preserved
We owe them all a great debt
"LEST WE FORGET"

Also let us give thanks
For those in the ranks
Who were returned home
Among us they do roam

Not asking to be glorified
As their actions were justified
Their mind, body and soul
Hiding how war takes a toll

History portrays them as a legacy
The young may show them empathy
But they can neither understand
Nor relive death in a foreign land

The way our ancestors undertook
Summarised on computer or a book
As their lives move forward
And age makes it awkward

They start to grow weary
Becoming mournful and teary
Reminiscing over wars cost
The brothers in arms lost

With memory beginning to fade
Dementia starting a cascade
For each day brings a new sorrow
As survivors see their last morrow

A Dementia Carer Poems

Life Chosen

The days are long and slow
Filled with heartache and woe
I sit alone and contemplate
My real true mindful state
Am I good or am I bad
Or just hiding happy and sad
Looking into a type of darkness
That is creating my blindness
To this life of absolute solitude
Due to the negativity accrued

The nights are proving problematic
With thoughts that are erratic
Living with a loved one's illness
Preventing us both from stillness
Their compulsions and obsessions
Along with their minds recessions
Causing a psychological war
My life becoming a holy chore
Whether decisions, right or wrong
I must forever remain strong

The weeks are spent in repetition
My only way to help this condition
Step by step we repeat our days
Trying to complete our mental maze
As we accomplish each new task
Hoping for answers to unmask
Clues I require for my clarity
So to prolong familial solidarity
Never letting the frustration control
And to stop it sapping at my soul

The months that have passed
Have given insight into the past
A life filled with regrets and blunders
Opening my eyes to the wonders
That I have left to go unseen
Since I was a confused teen
Looking forward into the future
Stitching a relationship with a suture
Knowing it can never be cured
Making sure each day can be endured

The years have made us both weary
But in my mind I can see it clearly
That we benefit from each other
Even if at times it feels like smother
Despite our relationship being rebuilt
My emotions awash with guilt
Over wanting to escape the stress
While looking for an easy egress
From this burden which is mine
Passed down to me through blood line

The life chosen to lead
Does not mean we need to accede
We are the creation of our fate
Until the journey to the fabled gate
What we do between birth and death
Is as simple as taking a breath
Only we can make it complicated
With an open heart it can be weighted
Towards a philanthropic inclination
Giving one's time to a beloved relation

Life's Highway

Travelling down life's highway
Without an exit or byway
One long continuous road
The mind beginning to corrode

When reviewing the past
It appears to have gone fast
For eight decades it has flown
Some flashbacks are unknown

A life of service he remembers
With a duty to family members
What has gone, never returned
Lost memories to be mourned

Over the years growing weary
Not thinking very clearly
The body wearing well
But mentally, he is in hell

As the illness takes hold
Reality begins to unfold
Nothing the same again
Dementia killing the brain

Nothing to look forward to
But the pearly gates queue
While living with this disease
Slowly decaying by degrees

Look Ahead

As I look ahead
My fears cause me dread
Waiting for the day
When I no longer have a say
Because he will not remember
That I am a family member.

He will look up on my face
Without recollection or trace
I will appear as a stranger
The one who is the arranger
No longer the son in his eyes
The blood bond in demise

I will start to see no awareness
Just a visual bareness
Communication without emotion
No love just remotion
His heart will appear cold
I know this is uncontrolled

The man I know is almost lost
This illness comes with a heavy cost
As my father dwindles away
He is not the only one to pay
Dementia may be his affliction
But it is also my infliction

Lost Lucidity

As the brain diminishes
Closer to life's finishes
The body begins to host
What is a living ghost

Old memories amassed
From back in the past
Subconsciously misrepresent
What is in the present

As the faculty withdraws
It creates faux pas
With family relations
In everyday situations

Day to day recollections
Going in negative directions
Hourly concentration lost
Is this illnesses cost

A lost lucidity
Impacts on the reality
Shackled and chained
A mind with dementia drained

Love's Dance

As his mind dance's through memories
His strong arms lifting with love
Twirling her around and around
Embracing a dormant passion
They both shall forever feel
But for a short moment in time
As her lost love descends
Beneath six feet of dirt
With one sudden death
Another's life dies too
Grieving upon her grave.
With only the memories of love's dance.

Then as the years slip by
His memory slowly fades
Obstructed by the mists of time
With age comes forgetfulness
Till she lives no more in his mind
The love that they shared
No longer remembered
Her face faded in to darkness
Their life together unclear
Left with only loneliness and fear
Trapped in an ever decreasing reality
With holes in the memories of his life

My Dad

As I look upon this old man
Once the leader of his clan
His life in a wrinkle and a line
The past remembered without a whine

Telling his soldiering stories
Reliving his former glories
Reminiscent of bygone days
Jubilant of his past ways

Remorseful at losing his wife
Joyful for the time of his life
Saddened when he feels alone
Thankful he has nothing for to atone

As his body wears well
His mind tends to dwell
The sands of time ravage
Causing unseen damage

Irritability begins to show
Frustrations increasingly grow
Loss of memory a blow
For such a man to fall so low

Dementia is a nasty illness
For which there is no forgiveness
Slowly taking away his life
Until finally he joins his beloved wife

Obsessions

As the soul carer I am troubled
With my daily tasks doubled
My thoughts, no longer my own
Living life like a robotic drone
Moving through each hour
Stress depleting my brainpower
Thinking for two, instead of one
Never knowing when I will be done
For all the love between two souls
Giving a reason for switching roles

Trying to comprehend the complexities
While overseeing his life's necessities
Taking each new day with a stride
Knowing deep down at least I tried
But still I struggle to understand
And feel I am drowning in quicksand
When his time and reality is lost
To what degree is our mental cost
With the incessant repetition, it's illogical
Although in his mind it's totally logical

Hiding feelings behind a forced smile
Constantly putting oneself on trial
Am I really doing my best?
Every move being second guessed
Should I give up and claim defeat
As each day I am on repeat
The same routine day in, day out
Filling me with endless self-doubt
While dealing with a loved one's obsessions
I am in dire need of counselling sessions

One's Mind

The depths of one's mind
Is a very organic kind
Electrical pulses flow
Through quick and slow
Pathways developed
Over time enveloped

From childhood evolution
To an adults dilution
As we grow older
Thoughts become bolder
Imagination diminishes
The closer to life's finishes

As people live longer
A need for care is stronger
Due to forgetfulness
Fear of loneliness
Loss of identity
Giving a sense of serenity

The one's afflicted
Have minds conflicted
Memories decaying
Simple abilities fading
Day to day repetition
Dementia killing recognition

Our Happy Days

I remember the happy days we had
Life as your son wasn't that bad
You always made my childhood fun
Even though I was chubby and couldn't run
My Christmases were exciting
Presents galore so inviting
As the years rolled in to adulthood
You looked on and nodded you understood
Letting me make the inevitable mistakes
Waiting patiently till I put on the brakes
Before passing on your wisdom once again
Knowing just how to dull my pain
In the fifty years since my arrival
You have always been my survival

Now please, let me take the lead
So I can help you to succeed
Your mind may be starting to yield
Without being able to be healed
Just know I am always by your side
As we fight on together with pride
This disease may be the winner at the end
But by your side I am your son and friend
Let us walk together towards life's sunset
Knowing death is no longer the threat
We will once again spend time having fun
Doing everything again as father and son
Until the day comes for me to say goodbye
When I will watch as you soar to the sky

A Dementia Carer Poems

<u>Peace</u>

There are days when I just stare
Thinking life is, so damn unfair
The people we love taken away
Little by little with every new day

There are hours of frustration
Trying to seek simple confirmation
Of what is going on within his head
To give me a clue of what's ahead

There are moments of pure madness
Culminating in a feeling of sadness
That I can and will never understand
What he experiences daily firsthand

There are times I see the person
That I love, before me worsen
A smile, a hug, even just a look
Then the disease is again the crook

There are nights when I am despaired
Sleep deprivation making me impaired
Due to his inability to settle and sleep
Making me want to curl up and weep

There are split seconds that I find
Myself wishing and praying lord, unbind
These heart ruled shackles and chains
And let us both fly off on separate plains

There are years of lost reminders
That used to be our special binders
Topics that made a conversational piece
Now all we have is an awkward silent peace

<u>Portal</u>

The portal of his existence
Capturing outsides resistance
As life now passes him by
Looking upon heavens sky

His chair by the window
Placing him in limbo
Wishing for an escape
From his mental rape

Reflecting upon his life
Dwelling on the strife
Instead of past glories
With fantastic stories

The experiences foretold
Are the burdens of the old
Locked away in a frail shell
His inner child trying to yell

An hour glass becoming void
The old man getting annoyed
As the sands of time run dry
His memories going bye-bye

Red Mist Forming

Resentment, building up
Isolation and frustration slowly killing
Sapping my dwindling willpower
Needing to release or escape

The red mist forming up above
Quickly descending to engulf
Eyes bloodshot with stress
Life becoming a total mess

Control and guidance at a loss
Violence likely resulting, if not stopped
As the mindless tension rises
Inanimate objects pounded

Language turning the air blue
Effing this and effing that
Verbally abusing everyone
No respect for anyone

Self-control a must
To survive and trust
Calming influences
Meditation practices

An open mind and caring nature
Instead of pet lip and immature
Kindness over irritation
Partnership, not manipulation

Red mist clearing with understanding
Conversation without blundering
Co-existing with each other in harmony
Treating family and friends properly

Resentment, dying down
No reason to distress
Willpower under control
Life back to normal I do hope

<u>Sands of Time</u>

Life in slow disintegration
With a mind in deterioration
Time is constantly devolving
While clock hands are revolving
Chasing hope hour after hour
Trying to control its power
From sunrise to sunset
With a feeling of regret
Sands of time ceasing to flow
Encapsulating the perpetual woe
That we are, but an apparition
In the picture of mental transition
Living our solitary meagre existence
Until there is no reason for resistance
The hourglass eventually runs dry
Leaving nothing more, but to cry
When dementia takes its toll
On the weak and weary soul
A life comes to an untimely end
The stories ending finally penned

Say a Little Prayer

At first everything appears fine
The sun will always shine
Illness is just a word
That everyone has heard
But dementia is hard to see
Just be prepared not to flee
Family will always be family
Even when they appear absently
Living within their own little world
Their angel wings still furled
What they want is understanding
Not labelling or branding
For they still want to be loved
Not a parent or partner unloved
So if a loved one is inflicted
And their life becomes restricted
Don't treat them any different
They may be scared or indifferent
As their mind starts travelling in reverse
It doesn't mean it's time for the hearse
Try spending a day in their shoes
So you don't have situations to defuse

A Dementia Carer Poems

When their condition begins to worsen
Remember they are still a person
Deal with each day as it comes
For they are still your dads or mums
Your husbands or wives with lives
Not people to be put in the archives
Let them be themselves always
Only control in sympathetic ways
That aids and cares through their daze
Making small gestures can count
As not been alienated is tantamount
To them feeling safe and secure
When you acknowledge there's no cure
But instead decide that love is pure
Even when they can't show it
Be sure you don't forget or quit
Just keep on loving and caring
Giving some time for sharing
Playing music to evoke the past
Singing to make memories to last
To bring them back from despair
And each day say a little prayer

A Dementia Carer Poems

Strangers

As each year slowly slips away
The mind follows day by day
For some it's only a little
Others, it's all ten skittles
Their life lost in one strike
Returning them to childlike
Every minute to be cherished
As the memory appears perished
The simplest recollections lost
Hiding the past in a misty frost
Leaving family and friends as strangers
Creating new complex dangers

An anxiety filled head
Accentuated feelings of dread
As the disease takes hold
Creating a mental blindfold
Sitting all alone unaware
With a blank lost stare
The family coping with stress
In a life full of distress
A loved one, in body only
Existing in a state of lonely
The brain in certain decay
Awaiting their own doomsday

Lucidity drifting in and out
Causing excess pain and doubt
Both carer and sufferer alike
For the sufferer, it's dreamlike
While for the ones who care
It's more of a waking nightmare
Never knowing what will occur
Stumbling through in a blur
Emotional mountains to climb
Taking each day one at a time
Being receptive of their needs
So some normality can proceed

Locked in a world of their own
Unable to let it be known
Replaying long ago, as if today
With thoughts going astray
Present events simply forgot
While yesteryears remembered a lot
Daily tasks cannot be performed
Without help for memory to be reformed
An absence of visual recognition
For the one doing the inquisition
No escape from the rigors of age
Trapped in their own dementia cage

A Dementia Carer Poems

Standing Before

The man I saw before me was a mystery
Even though we had a long history
Standing before this wooden symbol
I feel as small as a thimble
With the question of what we call life
That with it brings great strife
Never knowing when the end is nigh
As we gaze upon God's almighty sky
Mourning those, for who it is their time
Death's clock does its final chime
We come together to pay our respect
Chattering among us, we will reflect
Upon a loved one's mortal soul
As we make their life cycle whole
From birth to death we know the answer
That we will all become a cloud dancer
But today as we gather to honour you father
You created your own story in life like an author
Son, soldier, engineer, husband, parent and friend
Nearly ninety years of life you did blend
Unfortunately at the end your will was taken
By a disease that leaves the body forsaken
I am thankful, for today you start your eternal life
Hand in hand with your beloved wife
Please keep each other safe, till my time is done
And we are a family again, father, mother and son
So I stand here before you to rejoice and celebrate
Not for your death, for your life I commemorate
With love I see you on your journey
As you join God's celestial army

A Dementia Carer Poems

Sunday Bloody Sunday

Sunday is a day of rest
For those who are truly blessed
But for people who are carer's
It's just a day of mental terrors

There are ways for us to cope
A heart full of faith and hope
Whether through religious belief
Or meditation, however brief

This twenty-four, seven existence
Living two lives in coexistence
One as the selfless loved one
The other wishing it was all done

Thoughts of, what the hell
As the door shuts on the jail cell
Life turning topsy turvy, upside down
Overwhelming feelings of meltdown

No assistance, no guarantees
That you won't end up on your knees
Head in your hands crying aloud
While hiding under a shroud

The absence of solitude
Time to oneself, another daily feud
Who said caring was child's play
So much for Sunday, bloody Sunday

You may get the rest you need
When finally, you do concede
That you require some support
As long as it aids and doesn't thwart

The Old Man

The old man sleeps
While the young one watches

The old man dreams
And the young one prays

The old man reminisces
As the young one hopes

The old man stares out on what was
With the young one staring in with worry

The old man lives on in boredom
As the young one runs short of time

The old man so frail and weary of age
While the young one strong and supportive

The old man struggles to remember
And the young one struggles to forget

The old man tries his best to cope
While the young one shoulders the burden

The old man unable to manage
As the young one takes over as parent

The old man sees his son
And the young one sees his father

The world only sees a couple of men,
But never sees the love between them

Politicians have no answers to this
Question of the old living on much longer

The old are a forgotten generation
Unless the family takes control

My little rant is just that, a rant
As my words of caring fall on deaf ears

For society has no time or willingness
To help the elderly when they have a family

There Are Days

There are days of joy
And ones that annoy
Making decisions for two
Can make you feel blue
Deciphering words mumbled
By a mind lost and jumbled
In an existence of agitation
Creating constant aggravation

Then there are days of woe
As uncertainty begins to grow
With clarity being clouded
Certain faculties get shrouded
From the mists of the past
Old ghosts reappear amassed
To mystify and confuse
With visions to bemuse

When these days are done
No one will ever have won
For this illness has no cure
Just intentions, so impure
Destructive in its nature
Turning family into stranger
When it takes over control
Of the mind, body and soul

Prey these days never come
It will change your life's outcome
With everyday a merry-go-round
And no answers ever found
But if it does hit your parent
Remember nothing is apparent
A type of mental holocaust
That is the dementia cost

A Dementia Carer Poems

Through An Old Man's Eyes

Age makes him weary
Life drains away slowly
To bed he saunters
Ready to slip off to sleep

Age makes him irritable
Bored with what's left
Nothing to excite anymore
Ready to just leap

Age makes him forgetful
Struggling to remember
Memories so precious
Ready to store and keep

Age makes him sorrowful
Apologetic non stop
Always believing he is wrong
Ready to cry and weep

Age is not what's to blame
For some it's an illness
They try to compensate
As the dementia sets in

A Dementia Carer Poems

Trapped

As life stands still
Appearing in reverse
Spinning out of control
Freedom just a memory
Living life as a puppet
Told what to do and when
With your strings been pulled.

Once a proud, enigmatic beast
Now plucked from the wild
Caged and displayed
Like a cuddly, threadbare
Worn out teddy bear
Just longing to be held, hugged
And truly loved once more.

A strong, disciplined persona
With a mind trapped in the past
An exterior ever ageing
Reliving life as if in a loop
While waiting for the present
And maybe even a future
That will never catch up.

Struggling for an explanation
Awaiting answers wanted
Asking is this the end?
Where do I go from here?
What happens next?
As life folds in on its self
Like an immense black hole

With a look of bewilderment
Not sure of reality or dream
A feeling of immeasurable loss
Distress and disorientation
The simplest of tasks go wrong
This is what occurs with humans
As the body out lives the mind

Trial and Tribulations

Through trials and tribulations
The bond as blood relations
Takes a journey of ups and downs
Each day more repetitive rounds
A strain on those heart strings
That everything caring brings

Seeing a strong person drained
An old mind now unexplained
The day to day boring subsistence
Taking a toll on their very existence
With no means of resurrection
A constant feeling of rejection

Resigned to live out their days
In a dark and cloudy mental haze
Unsure of whether past or present
Existing in a depressive descent
No recognition of those so dear
Just a nervousness and a fear

Unable to perform a simple task
Their face becoming like a mask
As their natural abilities slip away
A price dementia makes them pay
Needing to be told what to do
Step by step guided through

The trial is the carer's sanity
When they realise their reality
And the tribulation is the illness
Which holds no forgiveness
While taking away forever more
The beloved person they care for

Twenty Four, Seven Caring

Time we have is sparse
Life can be a farce
Twenty four, seven caring
Is stressful and wearing

Half day a week free
Day care helps you see
A workout in the gym
Trying to help me slim

Destressed and serene
Is todays homely scene
A few hours to myself
The carer role on the shelf

Feeling guilty is tough
When doing my own stuff
Relaxing and writing,
Reading then rewriting

Then the doorbell rings
Retying the puppeteers strings
The carer within unleashed
Back to the life of a priest

All set for the weekly rerun
Playing the dutiful son
Over the next six days
As today fades to haze.

The time we have, we juggle
Life can be a struggle
Twenty four, seven caring
Is stressful and wearing

47

Twilight Confuses

When the dark sets in
Uncontrolled panics begin
No logic to the reason
But it is the season

When the skies go black
Memory goes out of whack
Sands of time undefined
Illness and shadows combined

As the dusk falls low
Thoughts will bestow
A sense of dread
Within the suffers head

Night time is foreboding
For a mind with bad coding
Creating paranoia within
Voices crying out therein

Twilight confuses
As the brain refuses
To control the feeling
That dementia is deceiving

Two Men

Two men face one another
One the father, a son the other
Over forty years of history
Between them, no mystery

Then as age takes a toll
A significant shift in role
The child becomes the parent
Familiar lines less transparent

In the son's eyes an old man
Needing him whenever he can
To help and give support
And be his father's consort

In the father's eyes a little boy
Playing with a favourite toy
Forty years stripped away
His memory in slow decay

The father of the sorrowful pair
Looks at the son with a stare
For a minute, a faint recollection
A family bond and connection

Tears of joy start to flow
A happy smile and the eyes aglow
Then in a single solitary breath
He returns to his living death

Stresses and strains on both men
Briefest memories now and then
Dementia's toll on father and son
In this battle unable to be won

Uncharted Frontier

From the darkness it appears
With a face full of fears
Unsure of what has happened
Only knowing life has blackened

A void that has been left
Gives a feeling of theft
That the past is lost forever
To relive it, is an endeavour

Trying to reach the guiding light
Which is constantly out of sight
Keeping one within the shadow
Away from all that is hallow

The deepest recesses of the mind
Thoughts and feelings declined
Pathways of unknown degradation
Leading to enigmatical castration

For the present to succeed
The dementia, must recede
Giving the courage to persevere
In the journey of an uncharted frontier

A Dementia Carer Poems

Unremembered

He can't remember
Losing a family member
His mother at four
A memory so sore

He can't remember
His very first mentor
On the stage at sixteen
Playing a foolish scene

He can't remember
Hot dry dusty weather
A uniform of green
Worn at eighteen

He can't remember
His day of splendour
When marrying his love
His precious turtle dove

He can't remember
A drunken bender
The birth of his son
After years of fun

He can't remember
How he had to surrender
The love of his life
His dearly departed wife
He can't remember
What to remember
The dementia consumes
Creating empty rooms

Vulnerability

When confusion does appear
It stems from the fear
Of not knowing his own mind
Memories mixed up and unaligned

Days and nights, indistinguishable
Time, no longer instinctual
The arms of the clock ticking
But in his head it's sticking

The boredom causes him to doze
When he wakes he needs to compose
Because his thoughts are jumbled
Within his reality which is crumbled

The present mixing with the past
Eighty years of memories amassed
His psyche in the balance
Causing his sanity to unbalance

A sense of loss that is felt
Nervousness cannot be dealt
Sudden thoughts of insecurity
Overwhelming majestic purity

From the depths of his vulnerability
To the extent of the fallibility
Nothing is actually his fault
As the mind resets to default

Weep Inside

The hours are long
I act so strong
But weep inside
As if I have died

The minutes tick away
Slowly each and every day
Life is complicated
And I am frustrated

Our minds do collide
Causing plausible divide
Bloods run cold
His illness takes hold

My heart is heavy
A burden so hefty
With serene behaviour
The role of a saviour

The internal struggle
A never ending juggle
Of patience and integrity
Accompanied by longevity

Through thick and thin
The relationship within
Creates inner turmoil
On this decaying journey

A Dementia Carer Poems

When

When we look upon life
With all its strife
Do we wonder why?
Things make us sometimes cry
From the good to the bad
And the happy and the sad
We all share a hope
That we can surely cope

When we look upon the person
Wondering how things can worsen
Their mind in confusion
Filled full of disillusion
With the past and present
Combining to misrepresent
Causing the unholy descent
Into depression and torment

When we look upon each other
Whether child, father or mother
A sadness will overwhelm
For we enter an unknown realm
Where a disease overtakes
Creating a life of sweepstakes
Will we be remembered?
Or family memories dismembered

When we look beyond tomorrow
All that can be seen is sorrow
A loved one slipping away
Slowly bit by bit, day by day
The person of our life's past
Disappearing from us, so fast
As the dementia takes hold
Where or when it ends is untold

Who Is Caring?

When everything appears lost
The families pay the cost
As the loved one slips away
Their memory starting to decay

What they see as logical
You see as obsessional
They see things you don't
And hear what you can't

Each day is a repetition
Same hourly conversation
To help and support
While trying to comfort

Keeping to a set routine
And never trying to demean
But keeping them so safe
From a world now unsafe

So do not be overbearing
With the person who is ailing
Refrain from despairing
As the loved one who is caring

Winter of his Life

As he enters the winter of his life
The sun setting on the end of days
Thoughts and memories jumbled
Reality twisted and contorted
Spring, summer, autumn and winter
Mixed together resembling chaos
Unsure of where or who he is
Simplest tasks appear difficult
The brain stagnant and befuddled
Boredom and routine the enemy
The person no longer resembled
Within the mirrors reflection
A face that is old instead of young
The body withered and drawn
Causing anxiety, panic and sorrow
Within this once handsome majestic man

With Life's End

To look back is to dwell
On a life being swell
Hoping it was lived well
And not a type of hell

Remembering the past
Memories amassed
Stories that are vast
To be told when asked

So before you're too old
Don't leave tales untold
Because life will unfold
And it maybe uncontrolled

Tell loved ones how you feel
Make the emotions very real
Do not hide or conceal
Let them know of your ordeal

For dementia eats away
And has a cost to pay
The memories will decay
So do not hesitate or delay

Because as time slips by
For the finally is to die
That you cannot defy
It's how you say goodbye.

We Will Never Be Done

I know we will never be done
As long as you are a loved one
Keeping you close to my heart
Looking up, now I see we're not apart
Knowing you're looking down on me
With a watchful eye from upon high

You may be gone from this earth
Still I feel us side by side
With your presence day and night
Wrapping me, within your warmth
Since I was a babe in arms
Keeping me, always safe

The day you left hurt like hell
Leaving a giant hole to fill
Not just losing you, dear father
But my best friend taken as well
God received a worthy angel
When your spirit finally soared

When the tears begin to flow
The heart still feels the blow
Of losing you over again
With an almighty chest pain
Memories, both good and bad
For you'll always be my dad

Holidays and birthdays never again
For to celebrate would be insane
Instead, every day I will thank
The stars above for the time we spent
With the North Star up above, twinkling
Passing on your message sent

A Dementia Carer Poems

I know we'll meet again
In a place there is no pain
Waiting for me in the light
Arms beckoning, telling me it's alright
Father and son, once again we'll reunite
Bringing us together within God's invite

Your Mortality is no More

As my year began, it was repetitive
Doing everything to be supportive
Then came the realisation
Life is formed with frustration
From birth to death is a long road
Where knowledge and experience is bestowed

As the year arrived half way
My life changed one Sunday
The reason being a bereavement
A sadness overshadowing an achievement
For a commitment that gave my life purpose
Was from me to him in earnest

As the year heads to a close
Life was on hold before, I suppose
The pain of loss still lingers
Like sand slipping through my fingers
Looking forward is hard sometimes
As if paying for unmentioned crimes

In the years that have past
I know that you never asked
So I gave my time and love freely
Not expecting the loss to hurt really
But you going, dealt a blow
Which has created a hole and a low

So if I am to survive the years ahead
I think I need to realise dead is dead
Then store away those sad memories
And use the happy ones as remedies
There to help my heart, once again sore
Now that your mortality is no more

A Dementia Prayer

Dear Lord

Hear my prayer of hope
Enable the afflicted to cope
Release them from their illness
Guiding to forever stillness
Deliver them from forgetfulness,
Solitude and loneliness
So that the mind remembers
Their dearest family members
Repairing their broken shell
Freeing them from a living hell
Giving back some dignity
In the eyes of holy trinity
Send forth a guardian angel
To accompany the faithful
From this devilish place
Towards heavens grace

Amen

A Dementia Carer Poems

Epilogue

What I would like readers to take away from my book of poetry is to remember people with dementia are still people. They still deserve a fulfilling existence with dignity and empathy above all else.

As a person suffering with dementia they experience everything as a mixed up jumble of thoughts and emotions. As their carer you can make their days easier by listening first, then act secondly with patience and empathy.

Remember three things when caring for a person with dementia:-

Look
Listen
Learn

Look at what they need or require to live life safely.

Listen to them talk, what they say can help you understand what their needs are better and most importantly get them to talk about their past using old photographs to prompt them as it is your family story they are telling.

Learn to read the signs, this can help you foretell if they are having a good or bad day, so you can react accordingly.

By putting the three L's in to practice you can help make their lives a little better each day and again remember the person they were before the disease, so you can help the person they are with the disease live their life to the fullest, but most importantly cherish every day you have with them as you never know when they won't be with you anymore.

Afterword

The person I cared for, who was my father passed away peacefully at the age of 88 on 2nd June 2019 at home in his own bed due to complications of the disease. In my heart I am filled with sorrow, but in my mind I am relieved. I am not relieved for myself, but for my father who I hope is in a better place where he is no longer suffering the indignity that dementia caused him.

A Dementia Carer Poems

Acknowledgement

A Dementia Carer Poems

Thank you to Steve Urwin and New College,
Durham for introducing me to the world of
creative writing and poetry.

Thank you to the Wishing Tree Writers Group
for giving me the confidence and support to
put my thoughts and feelings into print.

Made in the USA
Las Vegas, NV
03 May 2021